HE GUIDES US

Also by Jonathan Lamb

How to Survive as a Student (IVP 1985)

HE GUIDES US

Discovering the will of God

Jonathan Lamb

HODDER AND STOUGHTON
LONDON SYDNEY AUCKLAND TORONTO

All biblical quotations are taken from the New International Version of
the Bible unless otherwise stated

British Library Cataloguing in Publication Data

Lamb, Jonathan
   He guides us: discovering the will of God.
   – (Foundations) – (Hodder Christian paperbacks)
   1. Christian life
   I. Title   II. Series
   248.4   BV4501.2

ISBN 0 340 41072 8

CONTENTS

Foreword		7
Chapter 1	Hope for the future	9
Chapter 2	Knowing the guide	13
Chapter 3	Learning to trust	21
Chapter 4	Searching our hearts	26
Chapter 5	Renewing our minds	32
Chapter 6	God's word and God's people	37
Chapter 7	Gifts and circumstances	44
Chapter 8	The prophetic word	50
Chapter 9	Learning to listen	55

For Catherine and Becky.
May the Good Shepherd lead them both.

FOREWORD

When I was younger I envied those Christians who seemed to have a hotline to God. They appeared very confident in their assertion that 'the Lord told them . . .' As I have grown older, my own experience and the testimony of many other Christians have shown me that guidance is rarely that simple.

Discovering God's will can sometimes be a difficult process, and so I offer no instant solutions that can be applied to every situation. Often it seems that God intends that the process should not be easy, so that we learn a true dependence on him, and develop a mature faith.

The Bible brings both encouragements and challenges, both privileges and responsibilities, when it speaks about this subject. Consequently I have tried to answer three basic questions, which form the structure for this book.

First, what are the privileges associated with guidance? The first two chapters explain that the Bible emphasises the role of the guide, God himself, rather than the techniques of guidance. He is the one who has a plan for our lives, and promises his presence and his power.

Second, what are the conditions for guidance? In chapters three to five we look at some responsibilities we have to fulfil if we are to discover God's good and perfect will.

Third, what are the ways in which God guides? Chapters six to nine are devoted to some of the strands of guidance that God uses.

I must thank David Wavre of Hodder and Stoughton for his encouragement, David Mackinder for his sensitive suggestions at the editing stage, and also Clive Calver and Ian Barclay of the Evangelical Alliance for the invitation to contribute to the Foundations Series. I am committed to the work of the Alliance and gladly support the desire to present Christian basics in this way. I am, as always, deeply grateful to my wife Margaret who allowed me to escape to the Suffolk coast for a few days in order to write, and to Victor and Margaret Jack, whose flat at Sizewell Hall I was able to use.

Finally, special thanks to Liz Helyar who typed the manuscript quickly and efficiently, and to the extended family at Rockhaven who had to do more housework than usual while Liz slaved over a hot typewriter!

Personally, it has been a refreshment to remind myself that we can commit our lives to God with joyful confidence, knowing that he is the safest guide in the universe.

Jonathan Lamb
Belmont Chapel
Exeter
1986

1   HOPE FOR THE FUTURE

All good books – like good sermons – begin with a story, preferably funny! What follows is true, but sad.

A former colleague of mine was visiting the University of Kent at Canterbury. She was talking with one student as they strolled through an orchard near one of the halls of residence. The student stopped by a particular tree. She explained how a friend had committed suicide from that tree a day or so earlier. No one knew why. The only clue was an open book, left on her desk in her study bedroom. It was *The Castle*, by Franz Kafka. Much of this man's writing, in common with a good deal of twentieth-century literature, expresses the meaninglessness of life. It was likely that the student too had a deep sense of isolation and despair. She had nothing to live for.

No hope

This is one of the saddest results of a life lived outside of a relationship with God. The Bible describes this sense of hopelessness and lostness. People who are out of touch with the God who made them have no idea where they have come from, why they are here or where they are going. They are 'without hope and without God' (Eph 2:12).

This is certainly obvious among today's young

people. Whether or not they express it, there is a growing sense of pessimism and fear about the future. This is often to do with the threat of megadeath by radiation. Or it might be at a very personal level – no job, and nothing much to look forward to.

Substitutes

Without true hope, most of us turn to other things to plug the gap. There are all sorts of substitutes for hope.[1] Escapism is a prime example. Drug and alcohol abuse, or sexual licence, can be attempts to avoid facing up to ultimate issues. Self-indulgence – 'eat, drink and watch telly' – is another substitute: it tries to lessen the fear of the future by maximising on present experience.

Astrology is another substitute for hope which is becoming more and more popular. Whether it's Breakfast-time TV, the women's magazines or the daily papers, we can tune in and discover what sort of day we're going to have. And it's no game.

Take, for example, the business community in the United States. Many young professionals in their twenties and thirties, with well-paid jobs as Wall Street stockbrokers, bankers, lawyers and advertising executives, spend their lunch times patiently waiting in the Gipsy Tea Kettle in mid-Manhattan. They are there to have their fortunes told by 'psychic' tarot card readers, palmists, astrologers or numerologists – fifteen minutes of advice for seven dollars (plus tip).

In a newspaper article headed 'Career Tips on the Tarot Cards', Mary Dungan, aged thirty-six, a stock-broker with a large Wall Street firm was quoted, 'I go regularly to Joan Story to relieve my anxiety, reduce stress, and to give me a sense of control in my life. Psychics are more valuable than friends; they can see where you are going wrong and they give you hope for the future.'[2]

Most of us will understand this basic need to know where we're going. But all of these substitutes for hope prove empty in the end. They are short run answers to cope with the sense of lostness which characterises our generation.

From darkness to light

The person who lives in a relationship with God, the creator and redeemer, is in an entirely different position. He has a living and true hope. He has been taken out of darkness and brought into light. He is no longer without God and without hope. Instead, he knows where he belongs. He has come to know God, the Lord of the universe, the one who knows the end from the beginning. And he knows him as a Father and guide.

Knowing the guide

This is where we need to begin when we think about guidance. It's where the Bible begins. The subject needs to be seen in the context of this greatest Christian privilege – knowing the guide.

The one thing which gives meaning to life is knowing him. Jeremiah reported the Lord's message like this: 'Let not the wise man boast of his wisdom or the strong man boast of his strength or the rich man boast of his riches, but let him who boasts boast about this: that he understands and knows me . . .' (Jer 9:23–24).

It is this which makes sense of where we've come from, why we're here, and where we're going. To place 'guidance' in a box separate from the rest of our

Christian life is a mistake. Knowing God's will and knowing God are inseparable.

That said, the rest of this book will make sense only if we have come to know God as our Father. The most important thing about being a Christian is that we are in a right relationship with God. The Bible makes it clear that this is only possible through trusting Christ, the one who has opened the way into God's presence. John explains this in his gospel. Speaking about Christ he said, 'To all who received him, to those who believed in his name, he gave the right to become children of God' (John 1:12).

First, then, we will take a look at the privileges which belong to someone who is a member of God's family – someone who knows the guide.

1　　Stephen H. Travis *The Jesus Hope* (IVP 1974) pp. 15–20 lists and discusses (more fully than I am able to do here) seven 'substitutes for hope', some of which I consider below.
2　　*The Times*, Wednesday 5 March 1986.

2 KNOWING THE GUIDE

Being a member of a family has both privileges and responsibilities. Hopefully you're cared for, supported when things get tough and, despite the usual ups and downs of family life, feel that you belong. You might even be lucky enough to get breakfast in bed once in a while.

At the same time, you've got to pull your weight too if the family is to function properly. Since I'm such a poor cook, and my wife is such a good one, I always feel responsible to do what I like to think I *am* good at – washing up dishes.

All relationships are like that. And it's the same in God's family. If we are to know what God wants us to do, there are certain conditions to fulfil. We'll look at those responsibilities in the next chapter. But first, we'll begin with three privileges which we enjoy as God's children.

1 God has a plan for our lives

I wonder if you have caught the excitement of what this means. As a Christian, your life is tied up with God's plan and purpose, not only for time but for eternity! Life isn't meaningless or haphazard if you belong to God. You count for something and you're going somewhere.

Because God has drawn you into his family, he has

begun something in you which he *will* complete. In case
you're tempted to doubt it, take a look at how Paul
encouraged the Christians in Philippi: 'In all my
prayers for all of you, I always pray with joy . . . being
confident of this, that he who began a good work in you
will carry it on to completion until the day of Christ
Jesus' (Phil 1:4,6).

What is this 'good work'? What is God's plan for our
lives?

More like Jesus

Once again, Paul tells us straight: 'We know that in all
things God works for the good of those who love him,
who have been called according to his purpose. For
those God foreknew he also predestined to be con-
formed to the likeness of his Son, that he might be the
firstborn among many brothers' (Rom 8:28–29).

Please don't be put off by the theological words! The
key point is that God's overall plan for our lives is to
make us more like his Son the Lord Jesus. What better
plan could there be? He began the process the moment
we turned from sin and put our faith in Christ. And
he'll do the job properly. One day, when we see Jesus,
we will be like him (1 John 3:1–3).

John White, the American psychiatrist and Christian author, has written that God's plan 'has less to do
with geography than with ethics'.[1] He means that
God's first concern is not where we should be or what
job we will have (though he cares about these things, as
we'll see). His first concern is what sort of people we are
becoming. The process of making us what he wants us
to be, is more important than many of the issues we link
with the subject of guidance, which are about what we
should *do*.

Consequently, God's will concerns the whole of our

lives. When I talk with people about guidance they often have in their minds the key 'vocational choices': 'Should I get married? If so, how do I choose from all the eligible candidates?'; 'What church should I go to?'; 'Which job should I apply for?'

It's perfectly natural to focus on these questions, because they shape our lives so decisively. But God's will is bigger than even these things. His overarching concern is to make us more like Jesus.

Every step of the way

I want to underline that this is not to minimise God's deep concern for the smallest details in our lives. A friend of mine once explained that 'Every time I comb my hair, God has a recount'! He has biblical support for this (Matt 10:30–31). God is deeply committed to us and cares about the smallest thing.

But wherever we go, however disappointed we may be with our job or our relationships, or however frustrated by our personal failures, God's constant purpose through it all is to make us more like Jesus. He's not interested in guiding us about just one choice. He wants to be involved every step of the way in bringing about his perfect plan.

Nothing is going to take him by surprise. Nothing will foil his efforts or frustrate his purposes for us. God's plan for us has already been prepared: 'For we are God's workmanship, created in Christ Jesus to do good works, which God prepared in advance for us to do' (Eph 2:10).

The best!

Because it is God's plan, it is good and perfect (Rom 12:1–2). Accepting his will for our lives is therefore the most fulfilling and exciting thing we can do.

The evangelist Paul Little, who worked for many years among North American students, once said that he disliked the term 'surrendering to the will of God'.[2] To him it conjured up the picture of someone kicking, struggling, screaming and eventually confessing – 'OK! I'm caught – it's all over – I give up.' This comes from a distorted picture of what God is like. Paul Little continues, 'So many see God as a kind of celestial Scrooge who peers over the balcony of heaven trying to find anybody who is enjoying life. And when he spots a happy person, he yells "Now cut that out!". That concept of God should make us shudder because it's blasphemous!'[3] It is best summarised as a willingness to accept the will of God – and do so with confidence and joy. After all, this guide has our best interests at heart.

2 God promises us his presence

My wife and I once had to camp overnight in East Germany. Some weeks earlier, in London, we had booked a reservation at an official international campsite, on the outskirts of Leipzig. We crossed the border on Sunday, and drove to the city. Our petrol was getting low but we were pretty sure we'd make it.

Once in the city we began to follow the recommended route detailed in our international camping manual. Pretty soon we were lost in a maze of cobbled streets that did little for the van's suspension and even less for our morale. By now it was dusk. So we stopped and, in my limited German, I asked a passerby for directions. He had a rough idea where the campsite was located, and I did my best to follow his directions.

On the road again, the streets appeared to bear no

relation to what I thought he had said. We stopped and asked again. But once again the instructions proved inadequate. It was now dark, and the petrol gauge was indicating red.

Then we came across a couple. In my faltering German I made the same request as before. Their reply, though, made all the difference – 'We'll come with you.' And that's what they did. They sat in the van and led us through the ill-lit streets until we saw the gates of the campsite.

A guide is so much better than guidance!

The true companion

God hasn't despatched from heaven a book of rules entitled *How to discover God's will*. He's not some great computer in the sky, impersonal and distant, who, provided we feed in the right programme, will give us a daily print-out on what's coming up next.

Instead, he wants to be our companion. He wants to travel the journey with us. One of David's songs includes the Lord's assurances, words expressive of personal care and support: 'I will instruct you and teach you in the way you should go; I will counsel you and watch over you' (Ps 32:8).

A short while ago our second daughter was learning to walk. I would be a strange father if I had simply nudged her on the backside and said, 'Go for it Becky – have a crack at the Pennine Way.' All parents are alongside, supporting and guiding when their child takes its first steps. And David knew the Lord was with him in this way – God had his eye upon him. In another of David's songs, speaking of the man whose 'steps are established by the Lord', he expresses his confidence in the fact that 'the Lord is the One who holds his hand' (Ps 37:23,24 NASB). The psalmists were confident of the

Lord's presence taking them right into the gates of heaven (Ps 73:23–24).

That's what was so important for Moses. God had assured him: 'My Presence will go with you, and I will give you rest' (Exod 33:14). This builds into our lives a great sense of security and confidence. We might be tempted to fear the future were it not for the assurance that the heavenly guide is with us. Jesus put it simply when he described his relationship with us as a shepherd who knows his sheep, who loves them, calls them his own and leads them (John 10:1–18). It is this intimate relationship with God, through the Lord Jesus Christ, which is one of the unique features of Christianity: 'My sheep listen to my voice; I know them, and they follow me' (John 10: 27). Instead of worrying about how we can discover God's will, we should learn to enjoy the security of knowing that the shepherd leads us.

3   God provides us with his power

We've seen that the guide, instead of instructing us from a distance, is 'called alongside to help'. In fact, this is what one of the terms used of the Holy Spirit (the Paraclete) actually means. He is with us, and we therefore have all of God's resources available to us.

We've already seen that God has begun his good work in us, and that he will complete it. And so we come to a third great privilege for the Christian. God not only has a plan for us, and promises to be with us as we take each step, but he also provides us with all we need for the journey – he is a powerful God who is able to carry out his promises.

Partnership

Sometimes people misunderstand the idea of 'a powerful God'. I'm writing this chapter just a mile away from the Sizewell nuclear power station. I'd probably be locked up if I tried to sit next to the reactor and form a 'meaningful relationship' with it!

When we describe God as powerful we are not thinking of him as an impersonal force or a massive generator. He is our father. He has given us the Holy Spirit, who is a person. And it is in the context of a *relationship* that he carries out his work in us. In fact, we work *together*. Describing this partnership, Paul tells us how God brings about his purposes in our lives: 'Continue to work out your salvation with fear and trembling, for it is God who works in you to will and to act according to his good purpose' (Phil 2:12–13).

Basis for confidence

I hope that this chapter has shown that, when it comes to guidance, God has provided all we need. Since we have come to know the guide, he is removing our despair and hopelessness, and is replacing it with a sense of confidence, hope and joy.

These three privileges are the foundation for guidance, and I believe that, properly understood, they will take the strain out of the subject and bring a calm assurance whatever the situation or decision we are currently facing. All the questions aren't answered. But we come to the subject with a peaceful mind because we know that

* He has a perfect plan for our lives.
* He comes alongside us on the journey as a wise and compassionate Father.

* He is at work in us by the Holy Spirit to bring about his purpose of making us more like Christ.

Since God himself directs us, supports us and equips us, we can have every confidence that his plans for us will succeed.

1   John White *The Fight* (IVP 1977) p. 156.
2   Paul Little *Day by Day Guidance* (Falcon 1976) p. 13.
3   ibid. p. 12.

3 LEARNING TO TRUST

Therefore, I urge you, brothers, in view of God's mercy, to offer your bodies as living sacrifices, holy and pleasing to God – this is your spiritual act of worship. Do not conform any longer to the pattern of this world, but be transformed by the renewing of your mind. Then you will be able to test and approve what God's will is – his good, pleasing and perfect will.   (Rom 12:1–2)

These well-known verses about God's will point us towards our responsibilities – three basic conditions we have to fulfil if we are to discover God's guidance. Just as we have examined the great Christian privileges of knowing God – all to do with God's grace and mercy – so Paul has spent eleven chapters of his letter to the Romans doing the same thing.

And now, in the light of all that God has done for you, Paul says, this is how you are to live if you want to discover God's will. These three basic conditions are the focus of this and the next two chapters. They are to do with our character, our motives and our minds. The first condition, the subject of this chapter, is complete trust.

Total dependence

Not long ago I had my first experience of abseiling. I was hanging over a cliff on the west coast of Scotland –

not much of a drop, but quite enough when you're going down backwards! I learnt a number of lessons, but one particularly important one – you must learn to trust. You've got to trust the rope, and you've got to trust the person at the top doing the belaying. I can think of a better illustration of something I haven't tried (nor ever shall) – a parachute drop. There's no doubt at all that you are very dependent on your chute.

Learning to trust is never easy. For one thing, there is our pride. Being dependent on others is very healthy, and yet very difficult. You are educated to be self-sufficient and independent. But becoming a Christian, and then living the Christian life, is all to do with obedience and trust.

This is how Paul begins his appeal in Romans 12. If we are going to discover God's 'good, pleasing and perfect will', then the first condition is a commitment of our whole lives to him: 'offer your bodies as living sacrifices, holy and pleasing to God'.

David's confidence

I have just been reading all of the psalms attributed to David. It's surprising how many spell out this same condition for knowing God's presence, guidance and protection. Psalm 25 is a good example.

What is the basic attitude that lies behind David's request for guidance? It is an absolute and exclusive trust in God: 'in you I trust, O my God' (v 2); 'I take refuge in you' (v 20); 'my hope is in you' (v 21).

The reason David could say to God, 'I am ready to trust myself and my future to you', is that he'd seen something of God's character. He was sure that God wouldn't let him down. He knew something about God's saving power (v 5), his unfailing love (v 6), his goodness and justice (vs 7–8), and his faithfulness (v 10).

So his appeal for guidance is based on trusting someone he *knows*. As we've said, knowing God and knowing his will are closely connected.

On a human level, who do we trust? Back on that Scottish cliff, I was willing to go over the top because I knew my friend who was holding the ropes. I knew he had a sense of humour, but he wouldn't go so far as to let me drop. We trust people who are *trustworthy*, and that means we know their character.

Becoming like children

David's relationship with the Lord meant that he could seek the Lord's will with confidence. Whatever lay ahead of him, and however God led him, he was sure that God could be trusted: 'Show me your ways, O Lord, teach me your paths; guide me in your truth and teach me, for you are God my Saviour, and my hope is in you all day long' (Ps 25:4–5).

The same wise advice is given in Proverbs 3:5–6: 'Trust in the Lord with all your heart and lean not on your own understanding; in all your ways acknowledge him, and he will make your paths straight.' The clue to knowing the Lord's guidance is once again a childlike trust in God. Such trust has to be wholehearted (v 5), it turns away from human plans and secular wisdom (v 5), and it acknowledges the Lord's rule in every part of life (v 6).

Difficult questions

There will be times in our lives when God's will seems pretty mysterious. Why this happened? What can God be doing to put me through this?

Every Christian faces times like this, and it's as well to be honest about it. The psalmists certainly were. But if at such times we doubt God's *wisdom*, then our trust in God is deficient.

Or perhaps God's will seems uncomfortable. It's not what we would have chosen. If at such times we doubt God's *goodness*, then again we are not trusting as we should. David, like God's people throughout history, proved that God *can* be trusted to bring about his good purposes, however mysterious or uncomfortable his will may seem to be at the time.

Knowing and doing

Psalm 25 shows us, then, that a condition for guidance is the willingness to trust the Lord, accompanied by a commitment to do his will.

Because of my job I am quite frequently in the position of trying to find people to take on particular tasks. Most people can now tell when I'm sidling up to them in this way! And they usually express a *qualified* willingness when asked to do something: 'I'll do it for a month or two . . .'; 'I'll do it if someone else takes over my other responsibilities.' I don't blame them; I would probably say the same myself.

But we can never put conditions upon our commitment to do God's will. To *discover* his will and to *do* his will can't be divorced. 'Teach me your way . . . Provided it doesn't lead me *there*', is not on. Our willingness to obey must come first, if we're going to discover God's will.

This is how David describes it in Psalm 25:9: 'He guides the humble in what is right and teaches them his way.'

Humility, or meekness, doesn't get a very good press.

But it's a mark of a true disciple of Jesus, and we need to understand what it means. When Jesus said 'Blessed are the meek' (Matt 5:5), he used a word which was also used of wild horses that had been tamed. That is, it described great strength under control. The horse had been broken in; it could therefore be led.

Obedience and trust will grow as we deepen our knowledge and experience of the Lord. If we've come to know God recently, then we should learn to obey him day by day, as he reveals to us more about himself and his will.

This involves a willingness to accept God's will in *advance*. And it can be a problem for most of us. As Paul Little has pointed out, we tend to pray: 'Lord, show me what your will is so that I can decide whether it fits in with what I have in mind. Just lift the curtain a minute and let me see, so that I can decide whether I want to do it or not.'[1] But to think like this is to insult God. Do we really believe that his is a good, perfect and pleasing will? Do we really believe what we've looked at in the last chapter – that God's plans and purposes for us are only good, and that he *can* be trusted? If we do, then we'll be ready to accept his will, whatever it may be.

1   Paul Little *Day by Day Guidance* (Falcon 1976) p. ii.

4 SEARCHING OUR HEARTS

Guidance doesn't get any easier as we grow older. I've been a Christian for quite a few years (I should add quickly that I became a Christian when I was five), but discovering the Lord's will seems to be as difficult as ever. And I'm glad in a way, because it keeps me working on the first condition of guidance which we looked at in the last chapter – learning to trust.

I have to make a decision at the moment that will affect the next few years of my life. I've been asked to consider a post with a Christian organisation. It will put me in a more secure financial position, and it will take me around Europe, as well as other parts of the world. And both of these things immediately appeal to the wrong things in me. That's not to dismiss the job. It's simply that I've lived with myself long enough to know my weaknesses. And this, for me, is the most difficult part of guidance – testing my motives.

Searching our hearts

I began the last chapter with Paul's appeal from Romans 12. The second condition for discovering the Lord's will is expressed in Romans 12:2. The well-known paraphrase by J. B. Phillips puts it like this: 'Don't let the world around you squeeze you into its own mould . . .'

When it comes to guidance, one of the most important exercises to be conducted in God's presence is to be
honest about our motives. As David puts it in Psalm
139:23–24, we need to let the Lord search our hearts
and minds.

Why do we need to do this?

Every day we're under pressure to conform to the
world's value system: whether it be from the media, TV
adverts, our education or even our neighbours. And the
influence they exert can be pretty powerful. It can
shape our priorities, our assumptions, our values, our
ambitions.

There is, for example, a basic secular desire for status
or position or reputation.

Getting to the top

I once gave a young man a lift from Leicester to
London. Almost the entire journey down the M1 was a
monologue about his plans for a career in banking –
how he would go up one scale and on to the next; how
he would move around the country; how he would get
to the real positions of influence by his early thirties.
There is, of course, a right sense of ambition which
arises from a genuine desire to be a good steward of the
gifts God has given us. But there is also a subtle
temptation in our society to be governed by selfish and
ego-boosting motives – the desire to get to the top
whatever the cost.

Then there is that blind alley down which so many
people are rushing – materialism. Our decisions and
plans can be shaped by a basic desire for money and
possessions. We might be able to cover our tracks with
'spiritual' reasons for earning this, or buying that. But
if we're honest, we know we are succumbing to the

pressures of society rather than hearing the Lord's voice.

The short cut

We might be tempted to adopt another position which is common in our culture: going for the easiest course of action. We live in a *'Reader's Digest* world' where all the hard slog has been taken out of life. Everything's instant. And it's very tempting for the Christian to be influenced by this 'short-cut' mentality. That's not always God's way either.

A fantasy world

One final example. We can be influenced by what we might describe as romantic daydreaming. I suspect this is a more common activity than we imagine. Of course, it can come into play when we're thinking about who we'd like to marry; but it also operates when we're considering a career, or even what sort of Christian service we should be involved in.

Instead of facing a difficult decision or a particular pressure we have encountered, we're off on a romantic trip, fantasising about a job, a person, a possession, an appealing course of action. It's a form of escapism, of course, and it can paralyse us. We can be so immersed in this sort of daydreaming that we find it difficult to distinguish between the fantasy and the reality. And then it's very difficult for us to hear the Lord's voice.

Pleasing God

What was Paul's great ambition? He expresses it in this way: 'We make it our goal to please him' (2 Cor 5:9).

It is this which should become a filter on all our decisions. It becomes the real test of our motives. Not so much 'Will I be more successful?' or 'Will I be more secure, or have more influence, or be more happy?', rather, the question should be 'will it please him?'

The Lord Jesus spoke about our priorities too. He knew how we can so easily become preoccupied with the things which this world thinks important – possessions, time, places, preparing for the future. And so he gave us this simple test for our motives: 'Seek first his kingdom and his righteousness, and all these things will be given to you as well' (Matt 6:33).

God's will

This brings us to what, sadly, has become something of a cliché, but which, properly understood, is a vital prayer. We often use the words which the Lord Jesus himself prayed – 'Your will be done'.

If we genuinely wish to know God's will for our lives, we shall do no better than pray that simple prayer. At the same time, we will ask him to help us really mean it by purifying our motives.

This is an enormously liberating thing. Alec Motyer, writing about prayer in a commentary on the book of James, makes a helpful comment about the phrase 'Your will be done'.[1] He begins by asking whether or not we would pray if God was committed to give us everything we asked for. This might sound ideal – *everything* I asked for? That can't be bad! But wait a moment. It would assume that *we* know what's best. It would assume we knew what was coming up next week or next year. It would, in fact, be an intolerable burden to bear. We would probably never pray again. But the fact of the matter is that, in our weakness, we can seek

God's wisdom; and as we pray 'Your will be done', we are acknowledging that the Lord knows best. He knows the end from the beginning. This is why we can pray with confidence.

So to pray 'Your will be done', far from *imposing* a restriction on our praying, *lifts* the restriction of our own finite minds, our own short-run view, and our own sinfulness.

To pray this prayer with sincerity is to purify our motives. We are seeking his kingdom and his righteousness. We only want his purposes to be fulfilled.

God's priorities and mine

In 1906, a student studying engineering at Imperial College in London was given a small leaflet that was to change his life radically. The story of how God led him is an example of how motives are reshaped by God's priorities.

> He knew that his field of study held immense prospects worldwide, and he knew that his own ability was considerable. But the twopenny booklet struck at the very root of his assumptions . . . In momentous decisions in life there is a beckoning joy in God's gateways. The booklet spoke of losing one's life for Christ's sake; of dying in order to live. In short, it spoke of renouncing obvious plans and prospects because God had something better.[2]

This was the beginning of a series of events which led to a life devoted to effective missionary work in China.

Our real motive should be to please our heavenly Father. 'Delight yourself in the Lord', says David, 'and he will give you the desires of your heart' (Ps 37:4). This is because our will and his will come into line. We begin to share his concerns, understand what pleases him, and gradually learn to think his thoughts. And this leads us to the third condition which we must fulfil, if we are to know his will.

1   J. A. Motyer *The Message of James* (IVP 1985) p. 200.
2   Eileen Crossman *Mountain Rain – a new biography of James Fraser* (OMF 1982) pp. 3–4.

5 RENEWING OUR MINDS

I once was fortunate enough to gain a view of the Matterhorn in Switzerland which was unlike the typical scene on the picture postcards. I got as close to the mountain as I will ever get – by means of ski lifts, of course. Cloud hung around the famous pyramidal peak I'd studied in school geography.

Standing just beneath it, it appeared very menacing – bleak, grey, shrouded with mist. But from a distance, down the valley at Zermatt, it lost its terror. It looked beautiful. It was the typical picturesque view which appears on trays, handtowels, boxes of chocolates and anything else that can be retailed to the tourists.

So much depends on your perspective.

Our view of life

Francis Schaeffer once put it like this.[1] Either we are sitting in the 'naturalist' chair or the 'supernaturalist' chair; that is, we either look at life from the world's materialistic perspective or we view it from a biblical perspective.

To view life from God's angle is to live by faith. It means, as we've seen, that we take God and his purposes into account at every point in our lives. We believe he is the creator, the redeemer, and the one who controls the affairs of men. And we know he is involved in our own life.

Thinking straight

To think like this is to have a Christian mind. We cultivate God's perspective on life. As we have already seen from Romans 12:2, we aren't to think like the world thinks. We've been transferred from the kingdom of darkness to the kingdom of God's Son, and everything is different. We no longer share the world's ambitions or values.

So Paul brings us a third challenge – another condition for knowing God's will: 'Be transformed by the renewing of your mind' (Rom 12:2).

The whole truth

Instead of the values of this world shaping our thinking, and therefore our behaviour, God's truth must be the deciding factor. As the Holy Spirit renews our minds through the truth, we will develop a framework of thought which can judge the information we receive and allow us to take decisions, whether large or small, in a way which is consistent with God's will. Consequently, guidance won't be irrational. Let me give you an example to highlight the difference.

This is a true story of a student at a Bible college who was considering serving God overseas. He had some doubt, however, about where in the world God was going to send him. One day, he was shopping and, still wondering where he should work in the future, he happened to see some Brazil nuts in a shop window. When back at college he explained to his tutor that perhaps the Lord was leading him to go to Brazil. The tutor replied, 'It's a good job you didn't see any Mars bars!'

Thinking Christianly

We can't expect God to guide us through irrational
means – e.g., 'If the next car that passes me is blue, I'll
do this.' We are to use our *minds*. God is a rational God
who has made us in his image as rational creatures and
given us a rational revelation in the Bible.

Developing a Christian mind is not something expected just of brainy people. Every Christian has to
take it seriously. After all, we are all created with a
capacity to think, and this is part of what it means to be
truly human. And once we become Christians, we are
to be 'renewed in the spirit of [our] minds' (Eph 4:23
RSV). Paul says we are to cultivate 'the mind of Christ'
(1 Cor 2:16).

There are no short cuts in this process. As much as
we would like instant guidance, without too much
effort, the Lord doesn't usually work that way.

God's word and Spirit

Discovering his will can be part of the maturing process
as a Christian. It will mean being open to God's Spirit
by depending on him in prayer and thinking Chris-
tianly about the decision we have to make with a mind
that is informed by God's truth.

The psalm we looked at two chapters ago picks up
this theme: 'Show me your ways, O Lord, teach me
your paths; guide me in your truth and teach me'
(Ps 25:4–5).

How does God reveal his will? Through instructing
us. As we gain a deeper understanding of God's truth,
so we'll be able to make judgements in a godly way. In
other words, with the mind of Christ.

This is why John Wesley emphasised that God

generally guided him by presenting reasons to his mind for acting in a certain way. It was a rational process of decision-making. This is not to minimise the importance of the Spirit's work in our lives. But guidance is rarely a bolt from the blue.

A Quaker author, Hannah Whitall Smith, writing about religious fanaticism early this century, gave an example of a lady who had failed to understand this.

> There she tells of the woman who each morning, having consecrated the day to the Lord as soon as she woke, 'would then ask Him whether she was to get up or not,' and would not stir till 'the voice' told her to dress. 'As she put on each article she asked the Lord whether she was to put it on, and very often the Lord would tell her to put on the right shoe and leave off the other; sometimes she was to put on both stockings and no shoes; and sometimes both shoes and no stockings . . .'[2]

She had failed to see that God has made us with minds that are to be educated by his truth, and that much day-to-day decision-making is simply 'sanctified common sense'.

Knowing and growing

Paul's prayer for the Colossians was that God would fill them 'with the knowledge of his will through all spiritual wisdom and *understanding* . . . growing in the *knowledge* of God' (Col 1:9–10).

This will involve a lifetime commitment to developing a Christian mind through our reading of the Bible. This is the only sure way of discerning God's good, perfect and pleasing will. And this leads us to one of the

basic ways in which God guides us – a theme to which
we turn in the next chapter.

1　'Naturalist' and 'supernaturalist' can be slippery words
　　at the best of times. The danger is particularly acute in a
　　book on guidance. It is easy to see the two as opposites
　　and to exalt the more spiritual-sounding 'supernaturalist'
　　as a kind of Christian hooray word. Such is also a
　　temptation when we consider the use of words like 'natu-
　　ral' and 'spiritual': on the lips of rival factions in the
　　church at Corinth, for example, the use of these words
　　caused considerable acrimony – one set of explanations,
　　complete with favourite religious words, being vaunted as
　　better and more Christian at the expense of the other.
　　　　For our purposes, at the moment I am simply using
　　Schaeffer's illustration to make a single point about world-
　　views. In chapter seven, under the heading 'A practical
　　decision', I consider the pros and cons of 'spiritual'
　　explanations of guidance and in chapter eight I discuss
　　the place supernatural revelations might have in our view
　　of guidance.
　　　　For a fuller explanation of Schaeffer's illustration of the
　　two chairs see Francis Schaeffer *Death in the City* (IVP
　　1969) ch. 9, pp. 110–127.
2　Quoted in J. I. Packer *Knowing God* (Hodder & Stoughton
　　1975 edn) p. 264.

6   GOD'S WORD AND GOD'S PEOPLE

My shoelaces are always breaking. I'm usually stranded miles from a shop when it happens, and never carry a spare. It's my own fault, of course. I can tell when it's going to happen. Gradually the constituent threads of the lace begin to break (the eye through which it passes must be particularly sharp). One by one they go, and as the lace gets thinner I keep saying to myself that I must do something about it . . . until it's too late.

It's obvious that the lace is strongest when all the threads of which it is made are working together. When you're down to one or two threads, it's so weak that one enthusiastic tug means the end.

When we come to the *ways* in which God guides us, it seems to me that he usually employs a number of threads. They are interrelated and they support one another. It's unusual for there to be *one single formula* for discovering his will.

We'll look in the remaining chapters at some of these threads which God uses. No one thread on its own should be considered adequate, but we should look to them as a network of supporting elements through which we'll become sure of God's purposes for our lives.

God's word

When it comes to how the Bible guides us there is sometimes a little confusion. We may imagine that it can be used in an almost magical way.

A fellow leader in our church recently told me of a friend who went about discovering God's will in the following way.

If he had to make a decision, he would first express it in the form of a question. Then, when he came to the part of the Bible he was to read that day, he would count up the number of words in that particular passage. If there was an odd number of words, the answer to his question would be 'Yes'; an even number of words would mean 'No'!

This is obviously an abuse of the Bible, which has little respect for the way God has spoken to us or the way God has made us.

It is important to realise that there are two aspects to God's will. They are often described as his *general* will, and his *particular* will.

The broad canvas
His general will has already been revealed in the Bible, and applies to every Christian in every culture and every age. God's particular will is to do with those aspects of our lives where there is no specific instruction in scripture. We can see, then, that the vast majority of God's will has already been revealed to us. (See, for example, Eph 5:15–21; 6:6–8; 1 Thess 4:3–7; 5:16–18.)

God has spoken
A. W. Tozer used to say that we should never seek guidance on what God has already forbidden in the Bible; and neither should we seek guidance where he

has already said 'Yes'. In most other things, Tozer suggested, God probably doesn't have a preference, and he's pleased when we are pleased!

I'm not sure I would go quite that far, but I take his point. As we've seen, the Bible (if we read and apply it carefully) will give us clear guidance on our moral behaviour, our value system, our attitudes to work, money, sex, marriage, family life, church life, and much else.

Take your partners

Think for a moment about guidance for marriage. You could pin your hopes on a Bible verse – 'Go out with joy' (Isa 55:12), for example! But that wouldn't be the way to use the Bible. To begin with, as John Stott has written,[1] the Bible has given us a great deal of guidance about marriage:

* that it is God's good purpose for mankind, and that being single is not necessarily the rule but is a calling;
* that one of the main purposes of marriage is companionship;
* that a Christian man can only marry a Christian woman;
* that marriage is the context for sexual love and union.

But, as Stott goes on to point out, there are no details as to whether I am to marry Jane, June, Joan or Jemima.

Thinking God's thoughts

It is as we read the Bible that we come to know what God is like. We understand those attitudes and patterns of behaviour that he likes and that he dislikes. And increasingly, through the renewing of our minds in this way, we can apply these principles to the day-to-day decisions we have to make.

This is the broad backcloth for guidance: a mind

informed by the truth of the Bible. But is it the only way in which God uses the Bible to guide us?

The specific word

It has been the experience of many Christians that there are times when a particular verse or part of scripture speaks to them directly. What they read stands out as immediately relevant to their situation.

In the context of our regular and prayerful reading of the Bible, it seems that God is clearly confirming a particular course of action, or providing us with a warning or an encouragement. We might even find that on Sunday the preacher refers to it; or perhaps a friend reminds us of the same thing. I've experienced this, and wouldn't wish to dismiss its importance. But I'd want to add a word of caution.

For one thing, the Bible is not to be used in a random way, as we flip over the pages hoping that something will catch our eye that will guide us. For another, taking verses out of context and assuming they apply directly to ourselves has all sorts of dangers. (Another book in this series, Ian Barclay's *He Gives His Word* (Hodder and Stoughton 1986), deals helpfully with the question of how we read the Bible.) But perhaps most important of all, any guidance we believe God is giving us through such means needs to be confirmed in other ways. Other threads in the lace need to be there! Otherwise we'll be in danger of reading into a passage those things which will back up our preconceived ideas or personal preferences.

God's people

We began this book by thinking about some of the great privileges we enjoy as members of God's family. While we become Christians through *personal* faith, we immediately become a part of a new *community*. We are not on our own; we belong to a worldwide fellowship, and we should belong to a local fellowship too.

One way in which the world squeezes us into its mould is to encourage us to be self-sufficient. We don't need anyone else. And this can breed an independent spirit that rubs off on our Christian thinking. It sounds very spiritual to say 'God led me to do this', but if that means we imagine we have a personal hotline to God, and needn't check out our guidance with other believers, then we've got it wrong.

We need each other
The Bible is very clear about the need to turn to fellow members of the family for advice: 'The way of a fool seems right to him, but a wise man listens to advice' (Prov 12:15); 'Listen to advice and accept instruction, and in the end you will be wise' (Prov 19:20). This is one reason why God, in his wisdom, has put together a family of such diverse backgrounds, ages, experiences and gifts. We need each other, and God has specifically designed it that way.

Body life
The picture of the body which Paul uses to describe the Christian church clearly speaks about dependence on one another (1 Cor 12:12–27).

We should always seek out fellow Christians for their advice. It needn't be just when we have a major decision to make. It is important to be a part of a small group – perhaps a prayer triplet or a home group in your church – with whom you can be honest about how you're feeling, and where you need help. But it is particularly important when facing big issues to go to people who know the Bible, who understand human nature, and who know us – our gifts and our weaknesses.

Personal responsibility

We will still need very carefully to weigh the advice they give us. They don't make the decision for us, however wise they may be, or however forcefully they may express their opinion. No counselling or pastoral support must take away our own sense of account-ability and responsibility to God. We need pastoral support, but any leader who issues directions such that we feel the decision is out of our hands, is abusing his authority.

We have already stressed that it is the privilege of every believer to enjoy a direct relationship with *the* guide, the shepherd. Of course, we might make mis-takes; and other Christians might say 'I told you so'. But we will only learn to mature in our Christian life if we take personal responsibility for our decisions. We should always do so after taking the counsel of fellow Christians, including those in leadership in our churches (perhaps home group leaders or youth leaders), as well as our parents. Part of what fellowship in the body of Christ means is that we will benefit from this sort of support. And from time to time, we might be able to help others in this way too.

In it together

One final thing needs to be said about God's people and their role in guidance. The New Testament places an emphasis on *corporate* decision-making. The Lord guides his people as they wait on him together.

Here are some brief examples.

The church at Antioch was guided by the Spirit

while the believers were worshipping the Lord and
fasting. They sent Barnabas and Saul on a missionary
journey as a result (Acts 13:1–3).

The believers in Jerusalem came to a corporate
decision too: 'Then the apostles and elders, with the
whole church, decided to choose some of their own men
and send them to Antioch with Paul and Barnabas'
(Acts 15:22). There was also an encouraging note in the
letter they sent with them. It made reference to the fact
that, in coming to their decision, 'It seemed good to the
Holy Spirit and to us' (Acts 15:28).

Shared vision
I'm not sure that today we know too much about this
sort of corporate guidance. Perhaps in our church
prayer meetings, or when we're together as God's
people on a Sunday, we should be far more expectant
than we are, looking to God by his Spirit to join our
hearts and minds, so that we begin to share a common
vision and understand God's purposes for our life
together.

Certainly, as John Wesley said, 'There is no such
thing as solitary religion.' In the matter of guidance, as
in most other aspects of the Christian life, we need each
other.

1   J. R. W. Stott *Your Mind Matters* (IVP 1972) pp. 35–36.

7 GIFTS AND CIRCUMSTANCES

Gifts

These days it's usual for dads to be present at the birth of their offspring. If they don't pass out, they are sure to be deeply impressed by the miracle of birth. Just looking at tiny finger nails or a small turned-up nose is enough to soften the most hard-bitten cynic that ever entered the maternity ward.

In the beginning

God took an interest in us from day one. And I mean day one of conception, not birth. David, in describing God's intimate knowledge of every aspect of his life, recounted how God was at work even in his mother's womb: 'You created my inmost being; you knit me together in my mother's womb' (Ps 139:13).

God has been involved in our lives from the very beginning. We sometimes imagine that God ignored us until we became a Christian, and then he started to get to work. He gave us spiritual gifts so that, at long last, we really could be useful. But that is not so. As someone has put it, 'God is just as much sovereign of our genetic make-up, as he is of our spiritual endowment.' In other words, the way God has made us – with our particular gifts and personality – is a result of his special care and control, just as much as the particular spiritual gifts we may feel we have received since conversion.

Natural abilities

Of course we're sinful, and this takes its toll. Nevertheless, the natural abilities we have – whether creative skills, musical gifts, a caring disposition, love for children, and much else – are God-given. When we become Christians we don't necessarily lose these abilities. Instead, they are 'sanctified'; that is, they are turned towards the service of others and to the glory of God. Or at least they should be.

This is particularly important when it comes to thinking about the direction our lives should take. Our first line of thought should be to examine how God has made us.

Now it may be that, quite unexpectedly and contrary to what we might suppose, God has completely different plans for us. We might have thought that we were completely unqualified for a particular task, and that turns out to be the very thing to which God calls us. He's often done this to missionaries, for example. Gladys Aylward was turned down by a succession of missionary societies as being completely unsuitable. God thought otherwise.

Nothing is wasted

However, when we look at the way in which God guides, we can see how our previous experience, our natural gifts, even our failures, have been preparing us for a particular task.

Much of God's guidance, then, will unravel to reveal something which we might have expected. It will make good sense in the light of our natural make-up. As we have already seen, common sense is part of that natural endowment.

A practical decision

Samuel Moffatt, a Korean-born missionary, once gave his testimony at one of the large missionary conventions held for students in Urbana, USA. He explained how he was called to work in China.

> The decision to be a foreign missionary . . . is not a spiritual decision at all. Of course, to the Christian, all decisions are, in a way, spiritual. But my spiritual decision – the release of my own ambitions, telling the Lord that I was ready to go, sent me to North Dakota. Going overseas, going to China – there was nothing spiritual about that. It was a purely practical, commonsense decision. Where would I be most useful? Where was I most needed?[1]

Not all missionaries would see it that way. Some would feel that they needed a special sense in which the Lord was speaking to them about a particular work, or a particular country. And God deals with us all according to our different personalities and needs. The important thing to notice about Moffatt's decision is that much of guidance is to do with the prayerful application of common sense. As he illustrated in his address, imagine ten people are carrying a log, nine at the small end and one staggering at the heavy end. If you want to help, to which end do you go? This is what led him to serve the Lord in China.

Samuel Moffatt is not implying that a natural, commonsense decision is therefore unspiritual. He is simply exploding the 'super-spiritual' myth surrounding some views on guidance. A practical and sensible decision, made on the basis of obvious need, is in the fullest sense a spiritual decision if it is to do with the thoughtful and prayerful application of common sense.

A God of surprises

Once again, we must remember that God will usually work through several threads, rather than one isolated strand of guidance. Common sense is not enough. Indeed, there are dangers if we imagine we can sit at a desk and, in some exercise of business efficiency, briskly calculate God's will in the light of common sense alone. As we've seen, God may sometimes turn the whole thing on its head; he has the knack of using the most surprising people in the most surprising ways, 'to show that [the] all-surpassing power is from God and not from us' (2 Cor 4:7). Human wisdom won't always deliver the goods.

Circumstances

What clues can we gain from our circumstances, and what weight do we give them? This is another area where we need godly judgement.

Once again, common sense comes into play. Let me quote John White again: 'If I receive a letter from the Inland Revenue saying I have to pay five hundred pounds taxes, circumstances are guiding me to pay. If I am walking in the rain with my umbrella, I am being guided by circumstances to put up my umbrella.'[2]

We've already stressed the fact that God is in control. He is the sovereign Lord. We know that he is working in and through our circumstances. But how do we determine the way in which he is guiding us? This is a particularly difficult question when we are facing situations of pressure or difficulty.

Get going or give in?

A good biblical example is the story of the spies sent to check out the promised land (Num 13). The spies reported back with stories of giants, walled cities and large armies (although it was a very fruitful land too).

The majority of the spies drew the conclusion that circumstances were guiding them to go no further! But the two men of faith – Joshua and Caleb – knew that this was the *promised* land. God was leading them to press forward. These were circumstances to be overcome.

The same is true in our Christian lives. God's purpose is not usually to bypass difficulties, but to transform them. So, as White puts it, 'Circumstances are not the master of our fate.'[3] We need to pray for discernment in every situation, trusting that God's good purposes will be brought about.

At times this might be bewildering. Although I have stressed the fact that we are rational creatures, and our careful processes of decision-making (including common sense) are important in the task of discovering the Lord's will, we must always conclude by acknowledging his sovereignty. There will be times when we will face bewilderment, wondering why God has taken us along a certain path. True disciples, who follow the way of the cross, will inevitably face these questions. I conclude the chapter in this way because I believe it is a necessary caution. We should never imagine that we can chart out the whole of God's plan for our lives simply on the basis of our gifts or our circumstances. We will need the humility to acknowledge that we do not have all the answers; we are daily dependent on the guide.

1   D. M. Howard *Jesus Christ: Lord of the Universe, Hope of the World* (Downers Grove: IVP 1974) p. 100. This volume is a report of Urbana 1973.
2   John White *The Race* (IVP 1984) p. 148.
3   ibid.

8 THE PROPHETIC WORD

According to the Chinese, 'To prophesy is extremely difficult, especially with regard to the future'!

Is it possible today for God to intervene dramatically, and guide us in some supernatural way?

Do you remember the business of the two chairs – the naturalist chair and the supernaturalist chair (p. 32)? I mentioned that it is all too easy for a Christian to find himself back in the naturalist chair, looking at life from the world's perspective. To such a Christian, the suggestion that God might intervene in an extraordinary or supernatural way doesn't go down too well.

Variety

The New Testament shows that there were many ways in which God guided the early Christians. Very often the means was the process of decision-making which we have already looked at – minds informed by God's truth, and led by God's Spirit. A good example is the account in Acts 6, where a practical decision was taken with regard to the caring structures in the church. This was done through discussion and consultation, and a commonsense decision was finally made.

But there were other ways too. For example, in Acts 1:15–26 the story recounts the casting of lots as a means of guidance. In Acts 13, the first missionary journey began with the Spirit speaking directly to the leaders in

Antioch. While praying they were told to separate Barnabas and Saul for the work to which God had called them (Acts 13:2). Also in Acts we are told that Paul was guided by a vision (Acts 16:9).

Equally, it has often been pointed out that the second missionary journey began as a result of a heated division between two missionaries, and the development of two missionary teams as a consequence (Acts 15:36–41)! And much guidance for missionary strategy in the book of Acts did not appear to require supernatural revelation. Certainly supernatural intervention is clear, but we must be careful not to over-emphasise it – it certainly isn't an *essential* ingredient for discerning the Lord's will. But we cannot ignore the possibility that God might use these means in our lives.

A direct word

There is increasing interest today in the subject of prophecy and words of knowledge within the Christian congregation. The Evangelical Alliance (the sponsoring body behind this 'Foundations' series) has member churches which take a variety of positions with regard to these issues. Some churches believe that there is no biblical reason to suggest that such gifts were withdrawn with the apostles, and therefore they are to be experienced today. Other churches, equally committed to the Lord and to the authority of the Bible, believe that, with the closing of the New Testament canon, we no longer need such direct revelation. Still others would see that the prophetic gift is in operation today, but primarily through the powerful, Spirit-inspired application of the Bible, particularly through preaching.

If you are from a church which expects God to speak through the prophetic word, what role should

it perform in guidance? Let me make three general
observations.

Foretelling or forth-telling?

First, in the New Testament the primary purpose of
prophecy is *pastoral*. It is to strengthen, encourage and
comfort (see 1 Cor 14:3). There is surprisingly little
evidence of what we might call *predictive* prophecy – a
prophetic word which speaks of what is coming up in
the future. So we must be careful that we don't place too
much emphasis on prophecy as a gift which is necessary
for guidance concerning the way ahead.

Discernment

Second, it is important to notice how, when there was a
predictive prophecy, someone like Paul reacted to it.

For example, as Paul travelled on his way towards
Jerusalem for the last time, we are told that in every
place he visited he was warned in visions and prophecies that imprisonment and affliction awaited him (see
Acts 20:22–24; 21:10–14). The interesting thing is that
such words of prophecy didn't stop him from going. He
still felt the responsibility under God to hand over to
those needy Christians the relief money that had been
raised by the churches of Europe. Whatever function
the visions and prophecies performed – and they doubt-
less helped Paul prepare for what was coming – they
were not interpreted by Paul as guidance not to go.

Discernment is therefore needed in weighing up
prophetic words. The New Testament places an emphasis on the fact that prophecy must be weighed (1
Cor 14:29). As we have seen, in Paul's case, the prophetic word was not guidance from the Lord that he should

give up his plans to go to Jerusalem. This should caution us before we quickly jump to conclusions when we hear a specific word of prophecy. It may sound authoritative, but it needs to be tested and weighed, and we will need special discernment before drawing conclusions regarding guidance.

Check it out

This leads me to the third observation. As we have stressed, no one thread of guidance is sufficient on its own, and this is true of prophecy or words of knowledge. It would be unwise to base our decision for a particular course of action solely on a prophetic word. We will particularly need to gain the counsel of godly leaders as we seek to discern the Lord's will.

The story of the fleece

One of the themes I have tried to stress in this book is that God knows us and our needs, and he is able to provide for us all the way to heaven. He knows when we need his special encouragement.

Gideon was worried. Apparently God was convinced that Gideon was the man to save Israel from the Midianites. Gideon didn't really share the conviction. How could he be sure that God was speaking to him? Would God keep his promise?

He decided he could do with some positive sign. So he placed a sheepskin on the threshing-floor, and he said to God,

'If there is dew only on the fleece and all the ground is dry, then I will know that you will save Israel by my hand, as you said.' And that is what happened.

Gideon rose early the next day; he squeezed the fleece and rung out the dew – a bowlful of water.

(Judg 6:37–38)

The story goes on to show how patient God was. Gideon really needed to be sure. So perhaps God could run it again one more time. Except this time making the fleece dry and the ground wet. God did so. And Gideon got the message.

What lessons can we draw from this sort of divine intervention?

We walk by faith

One great lesson is to see that God understood where Gideon was at. He saw Gideon's weakness. He knew he was calling Gideon for a special job. And therefore there was a special need for positive encouragement.

Many of God's people can testify to these special moments of confirmation in their lives – maybe a letter, or a surprise 'coincidence', or a clear word of encouragement or exhortation. (There are some good examples in the book *When God Guides*, published by OMF (1984), which gives twenty-seven testimonies of the various ways in which missionaries have been led by the Lord.)

We thank God for his goodness in this way, but it would be a mistake to imagine that we can expect concrete proof of God's guidance for every decision we have to make. If it always worked this way, there would be little opportunity for the development of those mature characteristics of the Christian disciple which we have looked at already – a persistent trust in the Lord, a daily dependence on him, and a walking by faith, not by sight.

9 LEARNING TO LISTEN

It's fascinating watching kids grow up! One interesting feature is the selectivity they develop when it comes to their listening skills. They are remarkably well-attuned to adult conversation, however quiet, that makes reference (for example) to food! Yet persistent and loud requests from the parents to the child – 'Tidy that up'; 'Hold it with two hands' – seem to fall on deaf ears. Yet there's no need for hearing tests; the problem lies elsewhere!

Waiting on the Lord

When the Bible uses the word 'Hear' it often carries the connotation of not only receiving the information, but being willing to act on it. It implies listening with a firm purpose to obey. (Take a look at James 1:21–22.)

In these last few chapters we've looked at some of the threads that need to be held together in discovering God's will. We need to allow the Holy Spirit to change our minds as we read the Bible; we need the advice and support of fellow Christians; we take note of how God has gifted us; we carefully weigh up our circumstances, God's timing of events, and any direct word we may receive from the Lord or through his people. And surrounding it all is the assurance of God's good purposes for us, his presence alongside us and his power within us.

However much we may be aware of these supporting elements in guidance, there is one vital attitude that we need to cultivate: an ability to wait quietly on the Lord.

Most of us aren't too good at this. Life moves pretty quickly, and there are a host of distractions. Yet I want to conclude, as I began, by underlining the importance in our Christian lives of getting to know the guide, of learning to hear the shepherd's voice.

Growing up

One of the marks of spiritual maturity is expressed by David in Psalm 131. Some people call it 'a balanced contentment', and the nineteenth-century Baptist preacher C. H. Spurgeon once said that this psalm is one of the shortest to read but one of the longest to learn. In just a few lines, this song points to the process of growing into mature faith that is able to rest in the Lord and to wait on him:

> My heart is not proud, O Lord,
>   my eyes are not haughty;
> I do not concern myself with great matters
>   or things too wonderful for me.
> But I have stilled and quietened my soul;
>   like a weaned child with its mother,
>   like a weaned child is my soul within me.
> O Israel, put your hope in the Lord
>   both now and for evermore.

>   (Ps 131)

A sober estimate

If we are to hear the Lord speak through the varied means that we have looked at, the first thing we will need is humility. David could confess, 'My heart is not proud, O Lord, my eyes are not haughty'. And it was possibly because of the previous song (Ps 130), that David could express himself in this way. Psalm 130 is a personal prayer expressing the need for forgiveness and the importance of depending on the Lord:

> I wait for the Lord, my soul waits,
>   and in his word I put my hope.
> My soul waits for the Lord
>   more than watchmen wait for the morning,
>   more than watchmen wait for the morning.
>   (Ps 130:5–6)

The first place where this genuine humility will express itself will be in our praying. Unless we give time to this, we will be in danger of missing what the Lord has to say.

A peaceful heart and mind

David was also aware that one of the marks of mature faith, weaned from self-seeking and self-centredness, is the ability to leave some things in God's hands.

Every so often I meet Christians in their seventies or eighties, who display this quiet resignation at certain points – they've learnt that some things are 'too wonderful', too mysterious (Ps 131:1). Instead of being preoccupied with problems they find they can't solve, they display a peace of heart and mind that comes from resting in the Lord.

A cop-out? I don't think so. When Christians give their testimonies about guidance, it is surprising how often they refer to this sense of peace. They didn't know how their future was going to work out, but they were sure the Lord was in control.

This peace is often only won after a struggle! Paul refers to God's peace surrounding us and protecting us (Phil 4:7). But he prefaces it by explaining the hard work which is necessary if we want to experience such protection: 'Do not be anxious about anything, but in everything, by prayer and petition, with thanksgiving, present your requests to God. And the peace of God, which transcends all understanding, will guard your hearts and your minds in Christ Jesus' (Phil 4:6–7).

Quiet trust

The picture of the weaned child in its mother's arms (Ps 131:2) speaks of an important balance in our lives. The picture isn't of a sucking infant. Rather, David is referring to the still and quiet soul which is neither overdependent nor self-sufficient.

He had learnt to develop a quiet trust in God and his good purposes.

I'm not suggesting that we become totally passive. I have already hinted that knowing God's peace is usually experienced after expending some effort! Christian experience, according to the Bible, is often portrayed as a battle, and this is certainly true of prayer.

Security

David seems to hint at the right balance. We should avoid trying to take things into our own hands – our future plans and strategies – but equally, we should avoid an infantile faith in the Lord that we hope will solve all our problems and release us from the burden of thinking, discussing and choosing.

Rather, waiting for the Lord, putting our hope in him, is the pathway of prayer that will create a genuine peace in the face of decisions large and small. This comes from knowing the security of being loved by God, our Father and guide.

> Not merely does God will to guide us in the sense of showing us His way, that we may tread it; He wills also to guide us in the more fundamental sense of ensuring that, whatever happens, whatever mistakes we may make, we shall come safe home. Slippings and strayings there will be, no doubt, but the ever-lasting arms are beneath us; we shall be caught, rescued, restored. This is God's promise; this is how good He is.[1]

Second best?

God is the safest guide in the universe. We can lean hard on him and be sure that he won't let us down. He takes us as we are, not how we'd like to be or how others think we should be. He can even take the mistakes of the past and, because of his love and sovereignty, can shape our lives so that we are not doomed to 'second best'. We can be sure that he will take the clay and rebuild the pot once again into something useful and beautiful.

John Mark seemed to have messed things up when he became the focus for the argument between Paul and Barnabas. But the Lord restored him, and made him useful in God's work – even Paul was eventually to express his gratitude for Mark's ministry (see Acts 15:36–41; 2 Tim 4:11). And if you are not convinced by that example, remember the story of Peter – from denying the Lord through to effective apostleship.

God takes our mistakes and weaves them into his purposes of love, redeeming the past and making us more like his Son. No wonder we can trust him. He won't let us down. He'll bring us safely to our home.

Relationship

After everything has been said about the 'techniques' of guidance, and after all the manuals and books and seminars, it comes down to this basic relationship – the Father and his family, the shepherd-guide and his flock. God wants us to know him, and developing this friendship is the most important thing of all. To this end, we need to learn from the psalmist's example:

> I wait for the Lord, my soul waits,
>   and in his word I put my hope . . .
> O Israel, put your hope in the Lord,
>   for with the Lord is unfailing love
>   and with him is full redemption.
>
> (Ps 130:5,7)

1　J. I. Packer *Knowing God* (Hodder & Stoughton 1975 edn.) pp. 271–272.

HE GIVES HIS WORD

Ian Barclay

An Introduction to the Bible

The Bible is the one essential basis for all Christian belief: it is particularly important to evangelicals. Yet, too many take it for granted and accept or discount unquestioningly doctrines such as the infallibility of Scripture and biblical inspiration.

Ian Barclay challenges these assumptions and simply explains what the Bible is all about. He looks at how it was written, its authorship, its place and relevance in the lives of Christians today. He tackles the thorny problems of mistakes and contradictions. In particular, he shows how the Bible is still relevant and still speaks directly to us today.

Ian Barclay, an Anglican clergyman, is currently the Churches' Secretary of the Evangelical Alliance and the President of British Youth for Christ.

HE TELLS US TO GO

Ian Coffey

An Introduction to Evangelism

Evangelism: a highly emotive and often misunderstood subject, crucial to evangelicals, seemingly over-emphasised or even irrelevant and embarrassing to others.

In *He Tells Us to Go* Ian Coffey sets out to define – from a broad evangelical perspective – what evangelism is all about. Who is it aimed at? Should it be left to experts and professionals? What does the Bible teach and what does it leave unsaid? Is this a 20th-century phenomenon linked to the mass meetings of globe-trotting evangelists? Or is it strictly a one-to-one affair? What about the opportunities – and threats – of the media? How does evangelism relate to social action, to the ecumenical movement, to other religions?

Ian Coffey is a Baptist minister and is currently an evangelist with the Saltmine Trust. He writes a regular column in Buzz Magazine and is married with three sons.

WHERE TRUTH AND JUSTICE MEET

Clive Calver

Tracing the roots of Evangelical Belief

'An evangelical is a person who has committed his or her life to Jesus Christ, and seeks to live under his Lordship and authority, believing and accepting the Bible for what it says.'

Where Truth and Justice Meet defines evangelical belief and practice, sketches a short history of evangelicalism, surveys the current scene and calls for unity and social action, but above all for a continuing allegiance to the Bible as the foundation and inspiration of evangelical belief.

Clive Calver was Director of British Youth for Christ until taking up his present position as General Secretary of the Evangelical Alliance.

HE GIVES US SIGNS

Gerald Coates

Understanding the miraculous in the Kingdom of God

Gerald Coates bases this contribution to the Foundations series on his own testimony. He recounts with his usual verve and humour how he moved from scepticism to the belief that 'signs and wonders' were an integral part of living the Christian life today.

Drawing on the biblical teaching, Gerald Coates offers us an overview of the whole area of charismatic healing and associated phenomena. He provides faith-building examples and encourages the reader to be specific rather than general with faith-goals, and to claim the great promises and commands concerning the reality of the power of the Kingdom of God today.

Gerald Coates is the leader of a charismatic house church in Cobham, Surrey. As part of the Pioneer Team, he is actively involved in church planting and caring for a group of some forty churches.